CRACKING THE PRODUCTIVITY CODE

Jeri Miller

Legal & Disclaimer

TABLE OF CONTENTS

FOREWORD

I want to thank you and congratulate you for purchasing the book, "**Cracking the Productivity Code** – *Secrets to Improving Productivity Habits at Work*".

Productivity is a trait that we all want to develop as a person. Not only does it helps us do more work, but it also improves the quality of our work as well.

This book aims to help you in developing that productive trait. We will first take an in-depth look at the factors that makes us unproductive, as well as the dangers of Procrastination. We will also teach you the techniques on how to be more productive as well as give you inspiration to and reason why you should continue to be productive.

Thanks again for purchasing this book, I hope you enjoy it!

CHAPTER ONE
Your Status Identity at Work

A s a working adult, you have to admit that you spend most of your time in the office. You wake up early in the morning to get ready to head out and leave the office when the sun sets. Most of us consider the work that we had as the defining factor of our life quality as well as our identity.

Just imagine your answer when someone asked you the question "What do you do?" It is most likely that your answer to this question is your occupation.

But before we delve in further to the status of your identity in your workplace, let us first find out what identity really is.

> According to the famous dictionary, Merriam-Webster, it defined the term identity as "who someone is" and "the name of a person". It also defines identity as the "qualities, beliefs, etc. that makes a particular person or group different from others".

You may find out what your identity is by comparing yourself with other people, those people you feel that you are most different. In the workplace, no two people are the same. But at the same time, no two employees can be too much different with each other either. We all fall in some ways or another in a particular type of employee classification, which is based on the behaviors and actions that you exhibit while in the work place.

Here are the types of employees that you will commonly see in a workplace. Check and see if you fall into one or more categories of these types:

The Believer

The believer is considered to be the employer's ultimate dream employee. He is very much dedicated and committed to his work and loves his job very much. These kinds of employees are ready to give out all their heart and souls into their work. They are very much loyal to the company and the team that makes him the perfect leader as well as a member. They had a way to get their jobs done without putting too much effort. They also inspire their colleagues, and they try to give their very best to every job at hand.

The Soldier

The soldier is considered to be the most bankable type of employee. They are dedicated and committed to their work, and are sure to finish the task that they are given. The soldiers usually show an unwavering amount of loyalty to the company and you will find them sticking around their jobs for years. They are very much stable, but could be a tough challenge when faced with the prospect of change. They are great team players, though they lack the needed leadership skills. They lack the initiative to start something and most often rely to their leaders for their next orders.

The Champion of Ideas

These champions are most often eager employees full of new thoughts and ideas. They are the opposite of the soldier, they like to take initiative on something and are very much enthusiastic on kick starting new projects. These are the employees who like to think big; they always love to push their innovative ideas to fruition. However, these employees tend to have more difficulty staying in a single project for too long, most often they want to jump to another new project to give out their ideas instead. They are excellent in generating great visuals and they often see the bigger picture of a project, though because of this, they are most likely to miss out on all the little details.

The Climber

These are the employees whose main priority is to make it big and to reach to the top of the corporate ladder. These are the employees who are hungry for recognition and power. They are most likely seen with people who are important belonging in the upper tier as well as wanting to be involved in big, visible projects. These are the people who like to frequently hop jobs in wanting to reach to the top of the organizational hierarchy quickly.

The Flat Liner

They are the type of employees that are "just there", heading to the office just so for the reason that they need to go to work. They are just bidding their time while waiting for the next paycheck. They have no goals, no plan and most especially, no purpose. They do the least amount of work in a team and are always the first one out the door after the work hour's end.

Although they weren't really always like this, they may be among those new graduates who are just so eager to learn more in the corporate world, but had given up after the reality of the harsh world struck them. They are also the ones who stayed in the same company, in the same position for far too long that grew weary from all the disappointments and red tape of the corporate life. They have no initiative to change or take charge of new projects. Yes, despite all that, they stayed in the company just so to be able to receive their salary and benefits without any hassle.

The Virus

These are the type of employees that gives off the vibe of negativity. They are the ones who fuel gossip and starts conflicts with other employees. They take short cuts to make their work easier without regard to the company's policy and interest. They are most often impudent moody, and competitive. They will also be more prone to lying and blaming others for the mistakes they'll encounter, and if they had an opportunity conceal their errors they would even at the expense of the company.

The Doormat

They are the employees who were always pushed around and most easily targeted by bullies. They often ask others for sympathy, yet is not enough to help them out of their situation. The new people to the team are prone to being branded as one since they have the least experience.

The Wallflower

The wallflowers likes to stay hidden and under the radar. They are the ones who are the first to fade away once the task gets tough. They always fear that they might make a huge mistake or be tagged as some who is inadequate. So to avoid that, they stay hidden in the shadows, as they are too hesitant to take any kind of risks.

The OCD

They are the employees who are highly obsessive and compulsive. They are perfectionists, done in a bad way. They are the ones who fusses a lot over small things, something as simple as a punctuation mistake or the ones who are always rechecking the numbers in the spreadsheet. They are very much dedicated to their work, though excessively. Yet they exhibit the qualities of being relentless and tireless. Because of these qualities, they are the ones who are keen to keep their eye to detail.

Because most people go to their jobs almost every day, your job occupation can be a defining factor that people can use to find out who you really are. Though some may find it too unfair to be judged by people just by basing it on what they do to earn a living, and believe that the work that they are doing is irrelevant to who they really are as a person, but we cannot erase the fact that there are people living in this world who judge people just by basing it to the jobs that they had right now.

CHAPTER TWO
Reality Self-Check: Guilty or Not Guilty?

You may believe that you are giving your very best at work. You feel that you are quick to respond to the issues mentioned in your overflowing inbox, and that you are eager to attend all the meetings that require your attention.

But still, all your efforts are still not giving out the results that you wanted. You must wonder why your work isn't getting done, despite all the sweat and tears you have put into your work.

You may be ignoring problems that could dig deep and harm your performance if not answered immediately. You are most likely ignoring productivity problems that are silently sabotaging your work.

The productivity problem may not also revolve around you, but around your workplace as well. Your company could be very well a culprit of ignoring the productivity issues and problems that are occurring in your very own workplace. Your company might think that they know all the issues that are having a huge impact on their employees' productivity, yet they might be able to still continue to inflict damage to the productivity of their employees because they are overlooking some factors that could highly contribute to the work performance of their employees, even if these productivity problems is staring right in front of them.

So to find out if you and your company are looking the other way, here are the top ten productivity problems that are most likely you and your company is ignoring.

1. The Endless Meetings

Do you accept all the invitations for a meeting that comes into your inbox? Do you attend all these meetings, even if it doesn't really require your presence? Do you feel that you have accomplished something right after attending the meeting?

Attending meetings are the biggest waste of time everyone is openly partaking in a company. Almost everyone can call one, and they could take up most of your day. Most meetings have no agendas, nor is a follow up performed to ask for updates right after the meeting. Companies would be better off without these meaningless meetings. Do not attend all the meeting invitations that arrive in your inbox. Not all of them are necessary nor does it require your presence. Just choose the meetings that you feel that is relevant to the project that you are currently handling and kindly turn down the ones that doesn't necessarily contributes to the completion of your task.

2. The Chaotic Inbox

Do you live in your inbox? Do you rely on what you send and received in the email for the task that you needed to accomplish for the day? Do you spend the rest of your day sorting out and shuffling through your email?

Emails have become the equivalent for the old-world term of "paper-pushing", you feel that your job relies on the emails that you send and receive all throughout the day. You assume that by sending emails, you are finishing up your work, but on the contrary, no work has been accomplished by just sending out or receiving emails. Just set an hour or two per day opening up your inbox and discerning the emails that requires your attention to the useless ones. Promptly send and reply the emails during this time only. After that, go back to the task that you are finishing. This way, you won't be distracted to the constant checking and replying to these emails and you will actually get the real work done.

3. No Deadline

Does your boss fail to give you a deadline to your task? Do you feel that you are endlessly finishing up a task that seems to go on forever because you couldn't see the finish line up ahead to the task that you are currently performing? Are deadlines, more or less, just like guidelines in your work place and not really the date that the task should be submitted? Are you and your company too lenient and are prone to extend the deadlines, more often that it should be?

Deadlines are there for a reason. You and your company should really stick to the date that was given. You wouldn't be able to finish your work if you feel that, at the back of your mind, know that the date given to you as a deadline is just for show and that the work will be conveniently extended. You will become more lax in your work because of this, the quality of your work will drop as well as you won't be able to get any work done..

4. No Life-Work Boundaries

Do you feel yourself married to your job? Do you still think of your job even when you are at the comfort of your own home? Is your boss constantly calling you at your free days just for asking you for job related matters?

Employers should know where work ends and where their employee's life begins. They should keep themselves from calling out to their employees during their days off or making them work even if work hours are finished. Failure to do that could cause a huge amount of stress to an employee that could very well eventually lead to a burn out. What's worse in the corporate world today, is that majority of the companies that we had today thinks that working beyond the required office hours and those who sacrifices their personal life for work is a very admirable thing, even if the very act itself may destroy the employees in the long run.

5. Rewarding the Busy over the Productive

Do you feel more accomplished when you find yourself busy over simple, mundane tasks rather than really doing something meaningful and productive? As an employer, do you want your employees to look busy, rather than accomplish something for the day and relaxing at work after?

A lot of companies today are more likely inclined to reward an employee who looks busy. Because being busy is a very easy task to do, it would seem that something is being accomplished by being busy. But the truth of that matter is, no matter how busy you look, you may or may not accomplish anything by being busy. You could simply look busy by doing simple things yet not accomplish a thing. What is important is the amount of task finished after a day's work without sacrificing the quality. You could look busy by walking around the room or shuffling through your email or you could finish your required task in an hour, and relax afterwards. Which do you think will produce more work?

6. Late is Okay

Have you always arrived late in a meeting? Do you feel that it is okay to walk in a meeting 20 minutes late is okay, since the meeting wouldn't really start at the announced time?

Lateness should never be accepted as okay. Precious time is lost if you don't follow the time indicated in your meetings properly. Time should be spent on working on something productive and should not be spent dilly dallying because you feel that it is okay to come in late as no one would react violently if they saw you doing so. Employers should also be strict in implementing the proper time that employees should follow in their workplace, and should give corresponding penalty to those employees who failed the follow them.

7. Work Environment

Are you comfortable in your work environment? Do you feel uncomfortable and anxious in your work environment that you feel that you are not accomplishing anything because you feel discomfort in your workplace?

As an employer, your work environment greatly affects the ability of your employees to get the work done. A lot of companies today ignores this. They allow noise and clutter inside their work premises and fails to give adequate facilities for their employees. These factors could affect the effectiveness of your team.

8. Misguided Policies

Do you feel uncomfortable following your company policies? Do you feel the need to impose a lot of rules and regulations to your company just to keep your employees in check?

Senior management and HR loves to implement rules and policies without considering their employees and if it could affect their productivity. For example, one company implemented the no office walls policy. After three months of implementing the said policy, the whole team is in panic and couldn't get any work done, since they remove all office walls, they are unable to hold private conversations that would require only the key members of the team.

9. Technology Restrictions

Does your company prohibit you from using the telephone? Did they cut off the internet connection in your computer?

Technology is supposed to help and not to hinder you in your day to day work, as it would allow the employees to get more work done. And yet, even with the technological advancements of the world today, some employers are scared of utilizing technology to their advantage. They impose needless restrictions and inadequate tools, and acquiring systems that are simply not working and are out of date.

10. Reworking

Does your company still use strategies that are not really effective, yet still uses them because they are afraid to adapt to change?

Most companies fail to realize their mistake even after several attempts of doing it, since they are afraid to try out new strategies. If it fails for the first time, then most likely you will end up doing it over again.

CHAPTER THREE
Procrastination – One Silent Tsunami to Beat

Procrastination is a silent killer. The majority of people around the world practice procrastination to some degree, but there are people who are unable to resist the call of procrastination. It hinders them from getting something done, even to an extent wherein it could stop them from progressing in their careers.

To deal with procrastination, you must first recognize when you start procrastinating, try to fully understand why you start procrastinating, and take the necessary measures to prevent it from happening.

Before anything else, we must first understand what procrastination is.

Procrastination is the act or practice of carrying out a specific task with less urgency in preference over to the task that needed more urgently. It is also considered as procrastination if you do something that is more comfortable or enjoyable to do, putting off the tasks that needed to be done and deciding to do it at a much later time. Sometimes, the task will be done at the last minute, when the deadline is already near and impending.

The Impacts of Procrastination

As we are all guilty of procrastinating at some point in our lives, we should be wary of the effects that it has when you do it regularly.

Here are some of the damaging effects procrastination can cause:

1. **Losing Precious Time**

   Have you imagined how much time was wasted when you were procrastinating? Can you imagine the amount of time lost when you decided to put off the things that should be done?

   The worst thing that could happen when you are frequently procrastinating is when you realized that precious time has already passed. Before you knew it, a year, five or ten years have passed and you will ask yourself, what did you do for the past years? Where did all the time go?

   These particular feelings of lost and regret are something that no one would want to experience in any part of their lives. Humans don't have the ability to turn back the hands of time, and you will have no choice but to live a life full of frustration and regret, regretting the things that you should have done, but haven't because you procrastinated, wondering if your life would have been different if you have done differently.

2. **Missing Out Opportunities**

   Can you imagine how many opportunities you may have missed out on or wasted just because you didn't take the initiative to take the leap when they are yours to grab for yourself?

Those opportunities may have made your life a big difference, may it be for better or for worse, but because you were procrastinating and you put off doing things that should have been done in that particular moment, you missed it. A lot of opportunities only come once in your life, and there is only a very slim chance to be given a second shot at it.

3. **Not Meeting Your Goals**

The urge to procrastinate can come at you like a storm, bidding its time and coming to you in full force when you are in the process of thinking about your goals and the things that you want to achieve or change. Even if you have a strong desire to do something meaningful, it is very hard to take the first step towards it.

If you aren't that motivated enough, you might find yourself wondering why the things that you want in your life are very difficult to achieve. The answer to that question relies within yourself. You have to go deeper within yourself to break the barrier of resistance. We make goals that we aim to achieve because we always have that deep desire to do better in our lives. If you succumb to the temptation of procrastinating, then you likewise destroy the possibilities to make your life better.

4. **Ruining Your Career**

How you work can directly dictate the quality of the work that you produce, no matter how well you may have performed or achieve.

Check your work performance. Do you find yourself not meeting the deadlines or are you failing to reach your monthly targets? If you answered yes, see if the reason why you are failing to meet your targets is because you're prone to procrastinating. If that is the majority of the reason, imagine the consequence it will have on your career. Not doing well on your job could mean missing out on promotions. Worst case scenario, it may even cost you your job. Long term procrastination at work will ultimately ruin your career if you keep at it.

5. **Lowering Your Self Esteem**

There are some cases wherein one procrastinate because they have low self-esteem. If you think that low self-esteem might give you a pass to justify your procrastination, know that procrastination will only further lower your self-esteem. Being unable to start working on a job, you may even begin doubting yourself and asking if you are not capable of doing things.

It can destroy your life if you always hold yourself back. Low self-esteem could make you feel less that what you really are and it may further lead to acts that may sabotage yourself. Your confidence will slowly slip away if you continue procrastinating.

6. Making Poor Decisions

Making the decision while procrastinating can eventually lead to poor decision making. When you are procrastinating while making decisions, you will base the decision not because it is the right choice in the given situation, but because you need to make a decision because time is running out.

Procrastination can affect how we feel at the moment to a particular degree, and the decisions that we make are heavily influenced to the emotions that we are currently feeling.

7. Damaging Your Reputation

If you keep saying that you are going to do something, then because you procrastinated, wasn't able to do that thing, you are in turn ruining your reputation to other people. Remember that no one wants someone who can't keep their promises.

Aside from damaging your reputation, you are damaging your confidence and self-esteem at the same time as well. In time, you will find yourself sinking into the state of procrastination because you are not confident that you can do something anymore. People, in turn, would stop trying to depend on you or try to give you opportunities just because they feel that you are not up for the job.

8. Risking Your Health

When you procrastinate, you will somehow acquire stress and anxiety. It is well known that having too much stress in your system can affect greatly to your health. Procrastination can also lead to depression, which will affect the other areas of your life.

Also, when you procrastinate by putting your health checkups or exercise can also affect the status of your health. You may miss out finding an untreated illness or become unhealthy only because you try to put off doing things for the later.

Do not let procrastination dictate how you live. Beat this bad habit if you had a chance, do not let it overtake you.

Chapter Four
Rise and Shine – How to Have Productive Mornings

We all want to start our mornings right. When we have a fruitful morning, the rest of the day seems to follow through more seamlessly. Being productive during this time of the day doesn't just come and go without any exerting any kind of effort.

If you are not a morning person, this is most extremely difficult. It is hard enough to wake up in the early hours of the morning, but to force your brain to work without having the will and energy to do so sure is a pain for some.

To make your day right, here are some of the tips that you could use to get those productive juices running.

1. **Manage Your Energy**

    People are different in so many ways, most especially on how they differ and manage their energy. Some have a lot of energy during the morning, some have a lot of energy during the afternoons or evenings. Try to find out where your energy spikes the most during the day and plan the majority of your task to be done during that time.

2. Start Your Day Early

"The early bird catches the worm" - a famous quote that you may have heard about starting your day early. You should make it a habit to wake up early every day. If you have difficulty doing so, you could try to push yourself to wake up earlier than yesterday, even for a little bit. It may not be that super early, but at least you are training yourself to wake up early slowly but surely. But also remember that you should not deprive yourself of sleep while doing this, you still need to sleep at least 7-9 hours per day.

3. Plan Your Day

There are some who plans their day ahead the night before, while some plan their activities of the day during the morning itself. Either way, both are helpful to know what you need to do during the morning and all throughout the day. See what works for you the best.

4. Exercise After Breakfast

There is an interesting benefit that exercise aside from keeping your body fit and healthy. Did you know that exercising can generate and stimulate new neurons in your brain? It could also alleviate physical and mental pain on top of that. This means exercising can make you feel happy.

Although there is really no need to exhaust yourself in the morning from exercise, a simple 15-minute workout after breakfast will do the trick.

5. **Find Time to Meditate**

   Spending even at least 10 minutes every morning meditating can do wonders. You could do this right after you exercise in the morning to cool yourself down. Meditating have a lot of benefits. Relaxing can lessen your chances of acquiring arthritis and joint pain, can improve your immunity and hormone levels, and lowers blood pressure.

6. **Work in a Cool Place**

   Do you feel yourself sluggish and groggy when you are in a hot room? This is because heighten body temperature can make you feel uncomfortable and sweating. Try to turn down the temperature or move on to a cooler place to help your body and mind focus more.

7. **Create a Pre-morning Routine**

   It could be anything, drinking a glass of cold water, or reading the newspaper, or even doing your 10 minutes of meditation. This will be an action to kick start your day. This action will send routine signals to your brain, triggering them that it's time to start working. It can also make you overcome your lack of meditation to do something and help you get the things done even if you feel like you're not up to do it.

What you do in the morning is the indicator of how you will tackle for the rest of the day. The choices that you do every day determine the way we live our lives, the state of our health, and the quality of work that we create.

CHAPTER FIVE

To Work or Not to Work – This is Never the
Question

Whether you decide to join the workforce or not is entirely a decision you must make sometime in your life. But choosing not to work in an office doesn't give you a pass to not work at all.

Most people right after school finds themselves looking for work to be able to make money and earn for a living. Whether your objectives revolves in earning to pay off your debt, saving up on something that you want to buy, or even as simple to pay off your monthly expenses and bills, we all need to work our butts off in able to survive in this concrete jungle that we now live in.

We humans are beings with needs. We need the basic necessities like food, water and shelter to live. We need to pay our bills such as electricity and internet to live off comfortably. We need the pay off our luxuries such as expensive gadgets, clothes, jewelries, and such just to be able to satiate our wants. But we cannot achieve these all, if all we are going to do is spend the rest of the day lounging on the couch and sleeping all day.

Although the majority of the people around the world earn their living by working in a workplace, whether serving as a waiter in the service industry or a blue collared job in the office, or even as a laborer on a construction site, these jobs all have a hierarchy of positions and system one must live by when working in these kinds of jobs. Most likely, you have someone higher than you in terms of position, which gives you your daily orders and task to work on through the day. Not only will you need to finish these tasks that your boss has given you within the day, but you also need to maintain a harmonious relationship not only to your superiors but also with your co-workers as well. Working in an environment where you are not comfortable not only makes you unable to produce quality work on your part, but it also sabotages the chances of you moving on and up in the corporate ladder.

For those people who don't want to experience this kind of system and not opting to work for someone, that doesn't mean that there are no other ways to work yourself and earn for a living. We now have ways wherein you could earn money at the comfort of your own home as technology has enabled us to communicate with different kinds of people all over the globe. Technology has also developed so much that we now have jobs that centers and revolves around it, and these jobs could be easily done just by having a computer in your own home.

The most common jobs that you will see in the online world that earns really well are being a Virtual Assistant, Graphic Artist and Programmer. You can also earn a living by being a writer easily than before! Because the internet has open doors and opportunities for people who are freelancing for getting jobs and clients with much ease, it also has given a chance for people who only have a computer and internet at their disposal to earn money.

Do not make it an excuse that you cannot earn your living because you do not want to immerse yourself in the crazy corporate world. We now have a lot of ways to work aside from getting yourself a job outside. To work or to not work, this should never should be a question to be asked today.

CHAPTER SIX
Techniques on Redefining and Reformulating Productive Habits

Every one of us are looking for ways to be more productive in our day to day activities. Whether in our work or in our household chores, we aim to finish a lot of tasks in a day and being productive can push ourselves to finish and complete them.

Although it cannot be helped if somewhere along the way, we lost the track of being productive because we gave in to the temptations that surrounds us.

Especially right now in the digital age, where a lot of distractions come from our smart phone and gadgets, things that is now nearly impossible for us to part with. It is much harder to stay focused on a task because of this, unlike back in the days where there is no such technology available, and we could simply perform our tasks without having to constantly think if there is someone messaging us in our or sending emails to us. There are also no social media sites to check up on and see the updates of people who are connected to us. Life is simple back then, and productivity can also be easily achieved during that time as well.

To help you reclaim the almost lost art of productivity, here are some ways wherein you could install the habits of being productive.

1. **Cutting Your To-do List**

   Just because you want to finish a lot of tasks in a day doesn't mean that you have to cram all your tasks to be done in a single day. If you have 30 tasks in your to do list, you don't really need to finish all those tasks in one sitting. Try to cut off your to do list and do the things that are really important first before tackling on the rest in moderation.

2. **Take Breaks**

   Listen to your brain when it's screaming that it wants to take a break. Working for several hours without stopping can make your brain strain, using up all the glucose in your body. You can regain it by giving yourself a break: taking a stroll outside, eating lunch or snacking on your favorite sweets, or you could meditate. You will feel recharged and ready to take work head on when you get back.

3. **The 80/20 Rule**

   There is a rule saying that only around 20 percent of what you are doing in a day could only produce around 80 percent of the results. To achieve that, you must remove the things that don't relate to the task at hand, as they will only have a minimal effect on your overall productivity. Try to break down your task into steps and remove the parts that does result in minimal relevance until you will be able to come up with 20 percent of the task that will result in 80 percent result.

4. Focus on Yourself During Mornings

Checking up your email and calendar the first thing in the morning kills your productivity big time, as you allow other people to dictate the things that you must accomplish for the day. You can check in the earlier chapter on how to start your day right to have productive and meaningful mornings.

5. Tackle Difficult Tasks Before Lunch

Try to finish the challenging tasks first when your brain is still fresh and oozing with energy. If you have a meeting scheduled today, do it in the afternoon. By doing things this way, you will be able to be more productive in handling your time.

6. Create Your Own System

You may have already developed a habit that ruins your productivity over the years. You can prevent yourself from doing it again by developing a system. You can plan the hours where you will do a specific task.

7. Stop Multitasking

Stop yourself from doing 10 tasks in one sitting. Changing from one task to another without finishing them can drop your IQ at a slow rate. You can get things done more quickly and effectively by just focusing on a single task at a time.

Just because you are doing a lot of tasks, you can call yourself productive! Remember that less is more. Focusing on a single task and finishing it is key to being productive.

CHAPTER SEVEN
Free Productivity Tools You Can Use

There are a lot of productivity tools that you can find on the internet that could help you improve your work quality and time management. Though it is hard to sift thru the hundreds of programs and apps about productivity that could truly help you reach your goal.

We simplify the work for you as we give you these lists of free productivity tools that can fit your work personality and management type. Feel free to check them out.

For the Scatterbrain

If you are a type who has a lot of difficulty being organized, you can use these programs and apps:

- **Boomerang**

    It is a tool where it enables you to write an email now and send it later at a scheduled time. You can do this by clinking on the send later button.

- **Reqall**

    An app on your smartphone that acts as a virtual assistant. It remembers the tasks and things that you need to remember and organized them into the categories that you assign them to like notes, to-do list, shopping lists, and more.

For the Online Stalker

If you love to find out and research about your clients, customers, and new prospects, you can use these tools:

- **Rapportive**

    It could provide you with the needed additional information about a person in your email inbox such as his photos, his company, his location etc.

For the Obsession Compulsive

If you are an organization freak, then you have knowledge of where everything is located or placed, then this is perfect for you:

- **OfficeDrop**

    It can allow a user to scan any kind of document using his smartphone, and then later saves it on the virtual Office Drop Cloud server as a PDF where one could later grab and save on their own computer.

For the Delegator

If you are the type of person where in every little thing needs to be scheduled on your calendar down to the last minute:

- **Tungle Me**

    It can make you find your free time amidst all your schedules depending on your calendar activity, thus eliminating the risk of double booking a schedule with different appointments.

For the Social Media Enthusiast

If you are so hooked up in checking up your social media sites like Facebook then you can try this tool.

- **Docs For Facebook**

    It can let you create your office documents in your Web browser just like in your own computer such as Word, Excel and PowerPoint. You can then later share these documents to your Facebook friends.

For the Task Master

If you like to list your tasks, here are some tools that could help you

- **TeuxDeux**

    It is a tool to manage your to-do list. Its simple design makes it much easier to see your list, and if you missed doing a task, it automatically reschedules it for the next day.

- **Do**

    It is a simple productivity site and app wherein it makes you create your to-do list and assign it to other people. This is the perfect tool to manage a project with others.

For the Control Freak

If you want to take complete control of your task as well as others, then you could check this tool out.

- **Join Me**

    This program will automatically enable you to see another person's screen in an instant, no need for complicated sign up, you will simply need a special

URL. This way, you will be able to see what everyone in doing on your own screen.

<u>For the Insomniac</u>

Did you set up your computer to sleep the same time as you do, but you are doing an important task that doesn't permit you to do so, then this program is for you.

- **Insomnia**

  Insomnia prevents your computer running on windows to fall asleep. This is most especially helpful when you can't afford your computer to go to sleep right in the middle of doing a task.

CHAPTER EIGHT
Self-Assessment – Reading Signs of Changes and Improvement

Aﬀter everything that we have discussed from this point on, if you have followed the advice that we have given you to make yourself a better, productive person, then you will notice the subtle changes that may or may not occur in your body.

We all want to change for the better, not for worse. That is why we are all striving to change ourselves for the better, not only to improve ourselves, but to also improve the relationships that we have with the people around us.

Now, to know if you did change, even just a little, we have compiled a checklist to see if you did change for the better. Say a resounding yes if these signs apply to you:

1. Do you now write things down? Whether in meetings or gatherings, do you always bring a pad of paper and pen to write down the important things?

2. Have you now come prepared to any given situation? Are you now coming to the office and meetings right on time and you now have the tools that you need at your convenient disposal?

3. Are you now doing what you set out to do, what you announced you will do? Do people around you trusts

you that you will be able to finish the tasks that you have at hand?

4. Do you now regularly do follow ups after a meeting?

5. Are you able to maintain your workplace clean? Not neat, but tidy looking and professional? Are your files now organized and neat looking? Do you no longer have the difficulty of searching through your files looking for a specific folder?

6. Do you now prepare all that you needed for the day in advance? Do you always make it a point to get ready right before heading out to battle? Are you now confident enough that you could take on all the challenges that heading on your way because you are prepared?

7. Are you flexible enough to adapt to any kind of situation? Do you see the situation in all kinds of angles and adapt them to suit your style accordingly?

8. Do you now wake up earlier than you're usually done? Are you now planning your day ahead of time?

9. Do you now feel that you have a total grasp and control of yourself and your discipline?

10. Do you now take responsibility of your own life? Are you now able to understand the circumstances that you are in right now because of the wrong decisions that you may have made in the course of your life? Do you know seldom blame others when something goes wrong in your life? Are you now able to identify the wrong and do things differently the next time the same situation comes up in your life?

11. Are you now brimming with motivation and drive to do the things that you are set to do?

12. Do you now believe in yourself that you could do it? Do you enjoy accomplishing things, however big or small they may be?
13. Are you now striving to make yourself better continually?

If you say **YES** to most or all of these questions, then you can confidently head outside, ready to take on any challenges that comes in your way.

BONUS CHAPTER
NO! These People Did Not Succeed Lounging on their Couch

These people are successful in their own right. These people were able to reach the top due to perseverance and sheer will power. Their productivity habits also exude as well, helping them to reach their dreams and goals.

As a bonus for you all, here are some of the productivity habits used by famous people. Let it serve as an inspiration to you all to strive to be more productive. Who knows, you might see your name in this list in the near future.

Maya Angelou

Maya Angelou, the famous writer who won a Pulitzer Price, a Tony Award, Three Grammys, and many more awards, believed that work and home should be separate. She was so strict in implementing this that she even rented a small hotel room wherein she could write each day from 7:00 am in the morning till 2:00 pm in the afternoon. She also removed herself from other distractions. She also doesn't believe in multi-tasking. From the awards that she had managed to reap all through the years, one could say that this habit does work.

Ludwig van Beethoven / Ingmar Bergman

Beethoven and Bergman, both different from the industry they're in and in the era where they lived, both believed in rising early in the morning and working up until midday, and taking a break after. They strictly follow this schedule without any distractions.

Benjamin Franklin

Benjamin Franklin believed that it is necessary to record all your success and achievements for the day as well as also writing down their frustrations. This is something that he swore by, following his schedule every 9:00 pm by answering the question "What good have I done for the day?" It can help you prioritize your goals more and set up your goals for the next day.

Paul McCartney

Paul McCartney, one of the famous Beatles members, believed that he had to work through his limitations. The Beatles believe in the "10,000-hour rule", wherein they were able to perfect their music and art by playing more than 300 times per year for 4 straight years in the same German Concert Hall. Nothing can stop them from achieving their best, breaking through the limits that prevent them from doing so.

Barack Obama

The president of the United States of America firmly believes that he must eliminate the unnecessary decision that he needs to make in a day, like choosing what to eat for the day or what to wear for an event. His memos include only three options: Agree, Disagree, or Discuss Further. We could adapt this kind of method in our everyday lives by making our weekly meal plans or planning what we need to wear for tomorrow before heading to bed.

Mark Zuckerberg

The founder of Facebook makes it a habit of spending most of his days by reading various articles about successful people's habits on the internet. According to the people from Facebook, the young mogul can spend at around 70 – 80% of his time reading about the lives of successful people and even spend the rest of his hours at home reading articles and books about productivity.

CONCLUSION

Thank you again for purchasing this book! I hope this book was able to help you develop the productivity habits that you need in your life.

Developing the productivity trait was never an easy task to do. You need to sacrifice a lot of your bad habits and erase them from your system completely. This is to be able to fully adapt the trait of being productive.

We hope that you continue on being productive and apply it in every aspect of your life even after reading this book!

-- Jeri Miller